A WINE LOVER'S JOURNAL

With an introduction
& wine-tasting terms
by
Anthony Gismondi

RAINCOAST BOOKS

Vancouver

First published in 1998 by

Raincoast Books
8680 Cambie Street
Vancouver, B.C.
V6P 6M9
(604) 323-7100

1 2 3 4 5 6 7 8 9 10

CANADIAN CATALOGUING IN PUBLICATION DATA

Main entry under title:
A wine lover's journal

ISBN 1-55192-196-0

1. Wine and wine making – Miscellanea. 2. Wine tasting – Miscellanea.
3. Diaries (Blank-books)

TP548.w56 1998   641.2'2   C98-910412-5

Raincoast Books gratefully acknowledges the support of the Government of Canada, through the Book Publishing Industry Development Program, the Canada Council for the Arts and the Department of Canadian Heritage. We also acknowledge the assistance of the Province of British Columbia, through the British Columbia Arts Council.

Cover Photograph by Joseph Marranca (Digitally Altered)
Illustrations by Andrew Johnstone
Printed and bound in Canada

Contents

Wine Tasting:
From Heart to Finish

There is much more to wine than simply its colour, aroma (or "bouquet") and taste. Wine comes wrapped in history, geography, science and culture. It is as much about grape growing as it is about winemaking, and more than anything it is about people, both those who make it and those who drink it.

Looking back at my early notebooks, I am immediately transported to the kitchens and dining rooms of friends, where each month we would meet to taste wine. The brown bags, the nervous laughter, the earnest tasting and the inevitable guessing games have all become vivid snapshots of my early wine education. In a sense, getting to know wine is something akin to osmosis: each time you are exposed to the magic of the grape you absorb something else.

A Wine Lover's Journal is a unique record book in which you can not only chronicle the details of the wines you've tasted but also document the occasions in which the wines were enjoyed. So whether it is a magnificent feast, a momentous event or an intimate tête-à-tête, this diary allows you to record in detail those precious moments when good wine and good company create lasting memories.

Now that you have a place to record your wine-tasting

Only those who lack imagination cannot find a reason to drink good wine.

Anonymous

experiences you may be wondering which words to use to describe the various tastes you will encounter. Tasting wine is a subjective experience, so when you make notes about a wine it is important to use words that have meaning for you. Simply developing the discipline to write something down every time you pull a cork will go a long way to honing your tasting skills. And remember, it is important to have fun as well as to keep an open mind throughout the entire tasting process.

Evaluating the wine's appearance or colour is the first step in the tasting process. Vastly improved winemaking techniques make this assessment less crucial today simply because a wine's appearance or, more specifically, its colour, depth and clarity, are normally appropriate for its type and age. Remember that all wine changes colour with age. While red wines are initially violet, purple and bright red in colour, over time they will become orange, brown and, eventually, colourless. Similarly, white wine, which begins as bright green or straw yellow, will turn to a darker yellow and brown before losing colour completely. One caveat about colour: do not immediately associate deep, dark-coloured wines with top quality. While it is true that many of the world's great red wines are deeply coloured, there are many equally fine examples of pale-coloured wines. Once you've tasted a magnificent red Burgundy or a Portuguese Tawny, you will know what I mean. Colour is a better indication of age than quality and is perhaps best evaluated with this in mind.

Next up in the tasting process is assessing the aroma, often referred to as the "nose," of the wine. With over 95 percent of all wines opened and consumed 30 minutes after they are purchased, most tasters only smell the primary fruit aromas that emanate from young wines. In a well-made Chardonnay, the primary fruit aromas are often reminiscent of pears and apples. In the case of a Cabernet Sauvignon, it could be blackberry and *cassis*. Yet after several years of aging in a cool, dark wine cellar, the same Cabernet Sauvignon will take on scents of cedar, tobacco, mushrooms and leather. The Chardonnay will develop, too, taking on a richer, more complex, honeyed character. To evaluate the scents of a wine, simply swirl your wineglass to help release the aromas, then put your nose into the glass. If there are no unpleasant, off odours, such as rotten egg or a hint of sulphur (matchstick), you will be able to focus on and define the more positive fruit aromas, such as pear, apple, grapefruit, kiwi or what have you.

When it comes to tasting, small sips are the norm, but make sure you rinse your entire mouth with the wine. Again, lively fruit flavours are what you are looking for, along with a balance of acidity (the tart, lemony flavours that emerge along the sides of your mouth) and tannin (the dry, astringent flavours evident in the aftertaste of young red wines). The ability to identify specific fruit flavours, such as the black cherries of a Pinot Noir or the grapefruit/gooseberry aromas of a Sauvignon Blanc, or regional characteristics, such as the high-acid, refreshing, citric style of Chile's

Casablanca Chardonnay, comes with time, practice and discussion with friends of a similar mind-set.

Finally, pay attention to the aftertaste (or "finish") of a wine. Normally, the longer a wine lingers on your palate the better it is. As to whether you taste strawberries and your colleague tastes raspberries in a Beaujolais is a matter of experience and taste. Where you taste wine and with whom, along with which foods, completes the experience.

To get started all you really need is a sense of curiosity. I recommend that you try choosing a mainstream grape variety, such as a Chardonnay or Cabernet Sauvignon. For instance, a brief overview of the Chardonnay grape is easily accomplished by sampling wines from six different locales, such as Australia, Canada, Chile, France, Italy or the United States. Alternatively, you could simply investigate a California Chardonnay or, more specifically, any of those from the Russian River Valley of Sonoma County. Before long you will find yourself reaching for your copy of *A Wine Lover's Journal* each and every time you are about to taste wine. (I take mine with me wherever I go.)

This classic, beautifully packaged keepsake is designed to help you chronicle some of the information that you will absorb, although you are free to write as little or as much as you wish about any of the wines that pass your way. At a minimum, I encourage you to use the handy template to keep track of the nuts and bolts of any given wine, specifically its name, producer, the vintage or year it was made, the appellation or origin of the wine and its cost and purchase date. I can't tell you how many people I meet who wish they had written down the name of the "fabulous little wine" they had the night before. Making notes, even if it is just the name of the wine, its vintage and whether you found it agreeable, will make a good memory last even longer. To help you get started, I have provided a couple of sample entries at the beginning of the tasting pages.

Picture what the blank pages of this journal might look like a decade or two from now when they tell the story of not only the wines you've tasted but also the places you've been and the people you've met. After all, wine is about sharing experiences, which is why – thousands of years after it was first made – it remains one of the most civilized beverages in the world.

Anthony Gismondi

Wine makes every meal an occasion, every table more elegant, every day more civilized.

André Simon

Wine-Tasting Notes
& Experiences

Wine Notes

Wine	**Major Grape(s)**
B.C. MERITAGE RED	CAB. SAUVIGNON
Producer	CAB. FRANC / MERLOT
SUMAC RIDGE ESTATE	
Vintage	**Classification**
1995	V.Q.A.
Vineyard/District	
BLACK SAGE VINEYARD	
Region/Country	
OKANAGAN VALLEY, BC CANADA	
Date Purchased	
July 17, 1997	
Place of Purchase	
LIBERTY WINE MERCHANTS WEST VANCOUVER	
Price/Quantity/Volume	
$25 6 × 750mL	

Rating

Exceptional

Most Enjoyable

Drinkable

Poor

Tasting Notes

Colour/Appearance

MEDIUM-DARK, CHERRY-PURPLE, YOUTHFUL COLOR

Bouquet/Aroma

SPICY, PEPPERY, SMOKY, CHERRY AND BLACKBERRY AROMAS

Taste/Balance

SIMILAR STRONG BERRY FRUIT FLAVORS, WITH SOFT RIPE TANNINS

Overall Impressions

THIS IS A SOLID BC RED. I LOVE THE BALANCE OF FRUIT AND ACIDITY. ESPECIALLY IMPRESSIVE GIVEN THE YOUNG AGE OF THE VINES!

Tasting Experience

Date Tasted

LABOUR DAY 1997

Place

LIGHTHOUSE PARK

Occasion

MY BIRTHDAY

Tasting Companion(s)

SHELAGH, SANDY, BOO, ROBIN, BRIAN, MICHAEL, ELIN, JADE and AURORA

Accompanying Foods

OLD FASHION POTATO SALAD, CORN-ON-THE-COB, SPARE RIBS AND PEACH SHORTCAKE

Overall Memories

IT WAS A CLASSIC, BALMY WEST COAST EVENING. WE SAT OUT ON THE ROCKS UNTIL MIDNIGHT AND LISTENED TO SOME OLD JIMMY BUFFET TUNES. BRIAN BROUGHT HIS GUITAR AND WE ALL COUNTED THE SHOOTING STARS.

Wine Notes

Wine
CALIFORNIA CABERNET

Major Grape(s)
CABERNET SAUVIGNON

Producer
ROBERT MONDAVI WINERY

Vintage
1995

Classification
UNFILTERED

Vineyard/District
BLACK SAGE VINEYARD

Region/Country
NAPA VALLEY, CA
U.S.A.

Date Purchased
JANUARY 17, 1997

Place of Purchase
WINE HOUSE
SAN FRANCISCO

Price/Quantity/Volume
$ 30 12 x 750mL

Rating
Exceptional
Most Enjoyable
Drinkable
Poor

Tasting Notes

Colour/Appearance
DEEP, DARK, BROODING RED
COLOR.

Bouquet/Aroma
COMPLEX AND OPEN AROMAS OF OLIVES,
SPICES, BLACKBERRY JAM, SMOKE & TOAST

Taste/Balance
VERY INTENSE RIPE BLACKBERRY
JAM, CASSIS, VANILLA, BLACK PEPPER

Overall Impressions
LOVELY RIPE CALIFORNIA CAB.
VERY SUPPLE IN THE MOUTH.
DRINK NOW OR OVER THE NEXT
10 YEARS. VERY STYLISH.

> *It is better to have bread left over than to run short of wine.*
>
> ❦
>
> Spanish proverb

Tasting Experience

Date Tasted

Place

.

Occasion

Tasting Companion(s)

Accompanying Foods

Overall Memories

Wine Notes

Wine	Major Grape(s)
Producer	
Vintage	Classification
Vineyard/District	
Region/Country	
Date Purchased	
Place of Purchase	
Price/Quantity/Volume	

Rating

Exceptional

Most Enjoyable

Drinkable

Poor

Tasting Notes

Colour/Appearance

Bouquet/Aroma

Taste/Balance

Overall Impressions

Tasting Experience

Date Tasted

Place

Occasion

Tasting Companion(s)

Accompanying Foods

Overall Memories

Wine Notes

Wine	Major Grape(s)
Producer	
Vintage	Classification
Vineyard/District	
Region/Country	
Date Purchased	
Place of Purchase	
Price/Quantity/Volume	

Rating

Exceptional

Most Enjoyable

Drinkable

Poor

Tasting Notes

Colour/Appearance

Bouquet/Aroma

Taste/Balance

Overall Impressions

> *Good wine is a necessity of life.*
>
> ⊶⊰◈⊱⊷
>
> Thomas Jefferson

Tasting Experience

Date Tasted

Place

Occasion

Tasting Companion(s)

Accompanying Foods

Overall Memories

Wine Notes

Wine	Major Grape(s)
Producer	
Vintage	Classification
Vineyard/District	
Region/Country	
Date Purchased	
Place of Purchase	
Price/Quantity/Volume	

Rating

Exceptional

Most Enjoyable

Drinkable

Poor

Tasting Notes

Colour/Appearance

Bouquet/Aroma

Taste/Balance

Overall Impressions

Tasting Experience

Date Tasted

Place

Occasion

Tasting Companion(s)

Accompanying Foods

Overall Memories

Wine Notes

Wine	Major Grape(s)
Producer	
Vintage	Classification
Vineyard/District	
Region/Country	
Date Purchased	
Place of Purchase	
Price/Quantity/Volume	

Rating

Exceptional

Most Enjoyable

Drinkable

Poor

Tasting Notes

Colour/Appearance

Bouquet/Aroma

Taste/Balance

Overall Impressions

What is better than to sit at the end of the day and drink wine with friends, or substitutes for friends?

James Joyce

Tasting Experience

Date Tasted

Place

Occasion

Tasting Companion(s)

Accompanying Foods

Overall Memories

Wine Notes

Wine	Major Grape(s)
Producer	
Vintage	Classification
Vineyard/District	
Region/Country	
Date Purchased	
Place of Purchase	
Price/Quantity/Volume	

Rating

Exceptional

Most Enjoyable

Drinkable

Poor

Tasting Notes

Colour/Appearance

Bouquet/Aroma

Taste/Balance

Overall Impressions

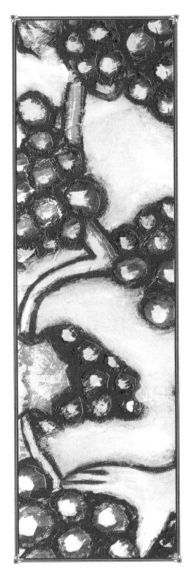

Tasting Experience

Date Tasted

Place

Occasion

Tasting Companion(s)

Accompanying Foods

Overall Memories

Wine Notes

Wine	Major Grape(s)
Producer	
Vintage	Classification
Vineyard/District	
Region/Country	
Date Purchased	
Place of Purchase	
Price/Quantity/Volume	

Rating

Exceptional

Most Enjoyable

Drinkable

Poor

Tasting Notes

Colour/Appearance

Bouquet/Aroma

Taste/Balance

Overall Impressions

> *From wine what sudden friendship springs!*
>
> —⊰◊⊱—
>
> John Gay

Tasting Experience

Date Tasted

Place

Occasion

Tasting Companion(s)

Accompanying Foods

Overall Memories

Wine Notes

Wine	Major Grape(s)
Producer	
Vintage	Classification
Vineyard/District	
Region/Country	
Date Purchased	
Place of Purchase	
Price/Quantity/Volume	

Rating

Exceptional

Most Enjoyable

Drinkable

Poor

Tasting Notes

Colour/Appearance

Bouquet/Aroma

Taste/Balance

Overall Impressions

Tasting Experience

Date Tasted

Place

Occasion

Tasting Companion(s)

Accompanying Foods

Overall Memories

Wine Notes

Wine	Major Grape(s)
Producer	
Vintage	Classification
Vineyard/District	
Region/Country	
Date Purchased	
Place of Purchase	
Price/Quantity/Volume	

Rating

Exceptional

Most Enjoyable

Drinkable

Poor

Tasting Notes

Colour/Appearance

Bouquet/Aroma

Taste/Balance

Overall Impressions

Tasting Experience

> *A meal without wine is as a day without sunshine.*
>
> ━━◈━━
>
> Louis Vaudable

Date Tasted

Place

Occasion

Tasting Companion(s)

Accompanying Foods

Overall Memories

Wine Notes

Wine	Major Grape(s)
Producer	
Vintage	Classification
Vineyard/District	
Region/Country	
Date Purchased	
Place of Purchase	
Price/Quantity/Volume	

Rating

Exceptional

Most Enjoyable

Drinkable

Poor

Tasting Notes

Colour/Appearance

Bouquet/Aroma

Taste/Balance

Overall Impressions

Tasting Experience

Date Tasted

Place

Occasion

Tasting Companion(s)

Accompanying Foods

Overall Memories

Wine Notes

Wine	Major Grape(s)
Producer	
Vintage	Classification
Vineyard/District	
Region/Country	
Date Purchased	
Place of Purchase	
Price/Quantity/Volume	

Rating

Exceptional

Most Enjoyable

Drinkable

Poor

Tasting Notes

Colour/Appearance

Bouquet/Aroma

Taste/Balance

Overall Impressions

> *Always carry a corkscrew and the wine shall provide itself.*
>
> —⊰◆⊱—
>
> Basil Bunting

Tasting Experience

Date Tasted

Place

Occasion

Tasting Companion(s)

Accompanying Foods

Overall Memories

Wine Notes

Wine	Major Grape(s)
Producer	
Vintage	Classification
Vineyard/District	
Region/Country	
Date Purchased	
Place of Purchase	
Price/Quantity/Volume	

Rating

Exceptional

Most Enjoyable

Drinkable

Poor

Tasting Notes

Colour/Appearance

Bouquet/Aroma

Taste/Balance

Overall Impressions

Tasting Experience

Date Tasted

Place

Occasion

Tasting Companion(s)

Accompanying Foods

Overall Memories

Wine Notes

Wine	Major Grape(s)
Producer	
Vintage	Classification
Vineyard/District	
Region/Country	
Date Purchased	
Place of Purchase	
Price/Quantity/Volume	

Tasting Notes

Colour/Appearance

Bouquet/Aroma

Taste/Balance

Overall Impressions

A bottle of wine
begs to be shared;
I have never met a
miserly wine lover.

———— ✦ ————

Clifton Fadiman

Tasting Experience

Date Tasted

Place

Occasion

Tasting Companion(s)

Accompanying Foods

Overall Memories

Wine Notes

Wine	Major Grape(s)
Producer	
Vintage	Classification
Vineyard/District	
Region/Country	
Date Purchased	
Place of Purchase	
Price/Quantity/Volume	

Rating

Exceptional

Most Enjoyable

Drinkable

Poor

Tasting Notes

Colour/Appearance

Bouquet/Aroma

Taste/Balance

Overall Impressions

Tasting Experience

Date Tasted

Place

Occasion

Tasting Companion(s)

Accompanying Foods

Overall Memories

Wine Notes

Wine

Major Grape(s)

Producer

Vintage

Classification

Vineyard/District

Region/Country

Date Purchased

Place of Purchase

Price/Quantity/Volume

Rating

Exceptional

Most Enjoyable

Drinkable

Poor

Tasting Notes

Colour/Appearance

Bouquet/Aroma

Taste/Balance

Overall Impressions

... with inimitable fragrance and soft fire ... wine is bottled poetry.

Robert Louis Stevenson

Tasting Experience

Date Tasted

Place

Occasion

Tasting Companion(s)

Accompanying Foods

Overall Memories

Wine Notes

Wine	Major Grape(s)
Producer	
Vintage	Classification
Vineyard/District	
Region/Country	
Date Purchased	
Place of Purchase	
Price/Quantity/Volume	

Rating

Exceptional

Most Enjoyable

Drinkable

Poor

Tasting Notes

Colour/Appearance

Bouquet/Aroma

Taste/Balance

Overall Impressions

Tasting Experience

Date Tasted

Place

Occasion

Tasting Companion(s)

Accompanying Foods

Overall Memories

Wine Notes

Wine	Major Grape(s)
Producer	
Vintage	Classification
Vineyard/District	
Region/Country	
Date Purchased	
Place of Purchase	
Price/Quantity/Volume	

Rating

Exceptional

Most Enjoyable

Drinkable

Poor

Tasting Notes

Colour/Appearance

Bouquet/Aroma

Taste/Balance

Overall Impressions

Great wine is a work of art. It … sharpens the wit, gladdens the heart, and stimulates all that is most generous in human nature.

H. Warner Allen

Date Tasted

Place

Occasion

Tasting Companion(s)

Accompanying Foods

Overall Memories

Wine Notes

Wine	Major Grape(s)
Producer	
Vintage	Classification

Vineyard/District

Region/Country

Date Purchased

Place of Purchase

Price/Quantity/Volume

Rating

Exceptional

Most Enjoyable

Drinkable

Poor

Tasting Notes

Colour/Appearance

Bouquet/Aroma

Taste/Balance

Overall Impressions

Tasting Experience

Date Tasted

Place

Occasion

Tasting Companion(s)

Accompanying Foods

Overall Memories

Wine Notes

Wine	Major Grape(s)
Producer	
Vintage	Classification

Vineyard/District
Region/Country
Date Purchased
Place of Purchase
Price/Quantity/Volume

Rating

Exceptional

Most Enjoyable

Drinkable

Poor

Tasting Notes

Colour/Appearance
Bouquet/Aroma
Taste/Balance
Overall Impressions

> *Quickly, bring me a beaker of wine, so that I may wet my mind and say something clever.*
>
> ❦
>
> Aristophanes

Tasting Experience

Date Tasted

Place

Occasion

Tasting Companion(s)

Accompanying Foods

Overall Memories

Wine Notes

Wine	Major Grape(s)
Producer	
Vintage	Classification
Vineyard/District	
Region/Country	
Date Purchased	
Place of Purchase	
Price/Quantity/Volume	

Rating

Exceptional

Most Enjoyable

Drinkable

Poor

Tasting Notes

Colour/Appearance
Bouquet/Aroma
Taste/Balance
Overall Impressions

Tasting Experience

Date Tasted

Place

Occasion

Tasting Companion(s)

Accompanying Foods

Overall Memories

Wine Notes

Wine	Major Grape(s)
Producer	
Vintage	Classification
Vineyard/District	
Region/Country	
Date Purchased	
Place of Purchase	
Price/Quantity/Volume	

Rating

Exceptional

Most Enjoyable

Drinkable

Poor

Tasting Notes

Colour/Appearance

Bouquet/Aroma

Taste/Balance

Overall Impressions

> *Wine cheers the sad, revives the old, and inspires the youth.*
>
> ━━◆━━
>
> Lord Byron

Tasting Experience

Date Tasted

Place

Occasion

Tasting Companion(s)

Accompanying Foods

Overall Memories

Wine Notes

Wine	Major Grape(s)
Producer	
Vintage	Classification
Vineyard/District	
Region/Country	
Date Purchased	
Place of Purchase	
Price/Quantity/Volume	

Rating

Exceptional

Most Enjoyable

Drinkable

Poor

Tasting Notes

Colour/Appearance

Bouquet/Aroma

Taste/Balance

Overall Impressions

Tasting Experience

Date Tasted

Place

Occasion

Tasting Companion(s)

Accompanying Foods

Overall Memories

Wine Notes

Wine	Major Grape(s)
Producer	
Vintage	Classification
Vineyard/District	
Region/Country	
Date Purchased	
Place of Purchase	
Price/Quantity/Volume	

Rating

Exceptional

Most Enjoyable

Drinkable

Poor

Tasting Notes

Colour/Appearance

Bouquet/Aroma

Taste/Balance

Overall Impressions

Tasting Experience

Wine … is a necessary tonic, a luxury, and a fitting tribute to good food.

Colette

Date Tasted

Place

Occasion

Tasting Companion(s)

Accompanying Foods

Overall Memories

Wine Notes

Wine	Major Grape(s)
Producer	
Vintage	Classification
Vineyard/District	
Region/Country	
Date Purchased	
Place of Purchase	
Price/Quantity/Volume	

Rating

Exceptional

Most Enjoyable

Drinkable

Poor

Tasting Notes

Colour/Appearance

Bouquet/Aroma

Taste/Balance

Overall Impressions

Tasting Experience

Date Tasted

Place

Occasion

Tasting Companion(s)

Accompanying Foods

Overall Memories

Wine Notes

Wine	Major Grape(s)
Producer	
Vintage	Classification
Vineyard/District	
Region/Country	
Date Purchased	
Place of Purchase	
Price/Quantity/Volume	

Rating

Exceptional

Most Enjoyable

Drinkable

Poor

Tasting Notes

Colour/Appearance
Bouquet/Aroma
Taste/Balance
Overall Impressions

Tasting Experience

Wine has lit up for me the pages of literature, and revealed in life romance lurking in the commonplace.

Alfred Duff
Cooper

Date Tasted

Place

Occasion

Tasting Companion(s)

Accompanying Foods

Overall Memories

Wine Notes

Wine	Major Grape(s)
Producer	
Vintage	Classification
Vineyard/District	
Region/Country	
Date Purchased	
Place of Purchase	
Price/Quantity/Volume	

Rating

Exceptional

Most Enjoyable

Drinkable

Poor

Tasting Notes

Colour/Appearance
Bouquet/Aroma
Taste/Balance
Overall Impressions

Tasting Experience

Date Tasted

Place

Occasion

Tasting Companion(s)

Accompanying Foods

Overall Memories

Wine Notes

Wine	Major Grape(s)
Producer	
Vintage	Classification
Vineyard/District	
Region/Country	
Date Purchased	
Place of Purchase	
Price/Quantity/Volume	

Rating

Exceptional

Most Enjoyable

Drinkable

Poor

Tasting Notes

Colour/Appearance
Bouquet/Aroma
Taste/Balance
Overall Impressions

> *Wine is the intellectual part of any meal … food is the material underpinnings.*

———✦———

Alexandre Dumas

Tasting Experience

Date Tasted

Place

Occasion

Tasting Companion(s)

Accompanying Foods

Overall Memories

Wine Notes

Wine	Major Grape(s)
Producer	
Vintage	Classification
Vineyard/District	
Region/Country	
Date Purchased	
Place of Purchase	
Price/Quantity/Volume	

Rating

Exceptional

Most Enjoyable

Drinkable

Poor

Tasting Notes

Colour/Appearance
Bouquet/Aroma
Taste/Balance
Overall Impressions

Tasting Experience

Date Tasted

Place

Occasion

Tasting Companion(s)

Accompanying Foods

Overall Memories

Wine Notes

Wine	Major Grape(s)
Producer	
Vintage	Classification
Vineyard/District	
Region/Country	
Date Purchased	
Place of Purchase	
Price/Quantity/Volume	

Rating

Exceptional

Most Enjoyable

Drinkable

Poor

Tasting Notes

Colour/Appearance

Bouquet/Aroma

Taste/Balance

Overall Impressions

If food is the body

of good living,

wine is its soul.

———✦———

Clifton Fadiman

Tasting Experience

Date Tasted

Place

Occasion

Tasting Companion(s)

Accompanying Foods

Overall Memories

Wine Notes

Wine	Major Grape(s)
Producer	
Vintage	Classification
Vineyard/District	
Region/Country	
Date Purchased	
Place of Purchase	
Price/Quantity/Volume	

Rating

Exceptional

Most Enjoyable

Drinkable

Poor

Tasting Notes

Colour/Appearance

Bouquet/Aroma

Taste/Balance

Overall Impressions

Tasting Experience

Date Tasted

Place

Occasion

Tasting Companion(s)

Accompanying Foods

Overall Memories

Wine Notes

Wine	Major Grape(s)
Producer	
Vintage	Classification
Vineyard/District	
Region/Country	
Date Purchased	
Place of Purchase	
Price/Quantity/Volume	

Rating

Exceptional

Most Enjoyable

Drinkable

Poor

Tasting Notes

Colour/Appearance

Bouquet/Aroma

Taste/Balance

Overall Impressions

> *Good wine, well drunk, can lend majesty to the human spirit.*
>
> ———❖———
>
> M. F. K. Fisher

Tasting Experience

Date Tasted

Place

Occasion

Tasting Companion(s)

Accompanying Foods

Overall Memories

Wine Notes

Wine	Major Grape(s)
Producer	
Vintage	Classification
Vineyard/District	
Region/Country	
Date Purchased	
Place of Purchase	
Price/Quantity/Volume	

Rating

Exceptional

Most Enjoyable

Drinkable

Poor

Tasting Notes

Colour/Appearance
Bouquet/Aroma
Taste/Balance
Overall Impressions

Tasting Experience

Date Tasted

Place

Occasion

Tasting Companion(s)

Accompanying Foods

Overall Memories

Wine Notes

Wine	Major Grape(s)
Producer	
Vintage	Classification
Vineyard/District	
Region/Country	
Date Purchased	
Place of Purchase	
Price/Quantity/Volume	

Rating

Exceptional

Most Enjoyable

Drinkable

Poor

Tasting Notes

Colour/Appearance
Bouquet/Aroma
Taste/Balance
Overall Impressions

Wine was born,

not invented....

Like an old

friend, it continues

to surprise us in

new and

unexpected ways.

Salvatore P. Lucia

Tasting Experience

Date Tasted

Place

Occasion

Tasting Companion(s)

Accompanying Foods

Overall Memories

Wine Notes

Wine	Major Grape(s)
Producer	
Vintage	Classification
Vineyard/District	
Region/Country	
Date Purchased	
Place of Purchase	
Price/Quantity/Volume	

Rating

Exceptional

Most Enjoyable

Drinkable

Poor

Tasting Notes

Colour/Appearance

Bouquet/Aroma

Taste/Balance

Overall Impressions

Tasting Experience

Date Tasted

Place

Occasion

Tasting Companion(s)

Accompanying Foods

Overall Memories

Wine Notes

Wine	Major Grape(s)
Producer	
Vintage	Classification
Vineyard/District	
Region/Country	
Date Purchased	
Place of Purchase	
Price/Quantity/Volume	

Rating

Exceptional

Most Enjoyable

Drinkable

Poor

Tasting Notes

Colour/Appearance

Bouquet/Aroma

Taste/Balance

Overall Impressions

Tasting Experience

> *Wine is the only natural beverage that feeds not only the body, but the soul and spirit …*
>
> Robert Mondavi

Date Tasted

Place

Occasion

Tasting Companion(s)

Accompanying Foods

Overall Memories

Wine Notes

Wine	Major Grape(s)
Producer	
Vintage	Classification
Vineyard/District	
Region/Country	
Date Purchased	
Place of Purchase	
Price/Quantity/Volume	

Rating

Exceptional

Most Enjoyable

Drinkable

Poor

Tasting Notes

Colour/Appearance

Bouquet/Aroma

Taste/Balance

Overall Impressions

Tasting Experience

Date Tasted

Place

Occasion

Tasting Companion(s)

Accompanying Foods

Overall Memories

Wine Notes

Wine	Major Grape(s)
Producer	
Vintage	Classification
Vineyard/District	
Region/Country	
Date Purchased	
Place of Purchase	
Price/Quantity/Volume	

Rating

Exceptional

Most Enjoyable

Drinkable

Poor

Tasting Notes

Colour/Appearance

Bouquet/Aroma

Taste/Balance

Overall Impressions

Wine lets no lover

unrewarded go.

———— ⫻ ————

Alexander Pope

Tasting Experience

Date Tasted

Place

Occasion

Tasting Companion(s)

Accompanying Foods

Overall Memories

Wine Notes

Wine	Major Grape(s)
Producer	
Vintage	Classification
Vineyard/District	
Region/Country	
Date Purchased	
Place of Purchase	
Price/Quantity/Volume	

Rating

Exceptional

Most Enjoyable

Drinkable

Poor

Tasting Notes

Colour/Appearance

Bouquet/Aroma

Taste/Balance

Overall Impressions

Tasting Experience

Date Tasted

Place

Occasion

Tasting Companion(s)

Accompanying Foods

Overall Memories

Wine Notes

Wine	Major Grape(s)
Producer	
Vintage	Classification
Vineyard/District	
Region/Country	
Date Purchased	
Place of Purchase	
Price/Quantity/Volume	

Rating

Exceptional

Most Enjoyable

Drinkable

Poor

Tasting Notes

Colour/Appearance

Bouquet/Aroma

Taste/Balance

Overall Impressions

No meal is ever
dull when there is
wine to drink and
talk about.

André Simon

Date Tasted

Place

Occasion

Tasting Companion(s)

Accompanying Foods

Overall Memories

Wine Notes

Wine	Major Grape(s)
Producer	
Vintage	Classification
Vineyard/District	
Region/Country	
Date Purchased	
Place of Purchase	
Price/Quantity/Volume	

Rating

Exceptional

Most Enjoyable

Drinkable

Poor

Tasting Notes

Colour/Appearance

Bouquet/Aroma

Taste/Balance

Overall Impressions

Tasting Experience

Date Tasted

Place

Occasion

Tasting Companion(s)

Accompanying Foods

Overall Memories

Wine Notes

Wine	Major Grape(s)
Producer	
Vintage	Classification
Vineyard/District	
Region/Country	
Date Purchased	
Place of Purchase	
Price/Quantity/Volume	

Rating

Exceptional

Most Enjoyable

Drinkable

Poor

Tasting Notes

Colour/Appearance

Bouquet/Aroma

Taste/Balance

Overall Impressions

A bottle of good wine, like a good act, shines ever in the retrospect.

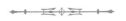

Robert Louis Stevenson

Tasting Experience

Date Tasted

Place

Occasion

Tasting Companion(s)

Accompanying Foods

Overall Memories

Wine Notes

Wine	Major Grape(s)
Producer	
Vintage	Classification
Vineyard/District	
Region/Country	
Date Purchased	
Place of Purchase	
Overall Impressions	
Price/Quantity/Volume	

Rating

Exceptional

Most Enjoyable

Drinkable

Poor

Tasting Notes

Colour/Appearance
Bouquet/Aroma
Taste/Balance
Overall Impressions

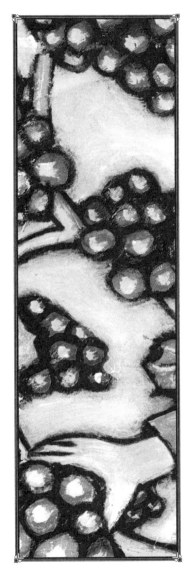

Tasting Experience

Date Tasted

Place

Occasion

Tasting Companion(s)

Accompanying Foods

Overall Memories

Wines to Try Next Time

A waltz and a glass of wine invite an encore.

Johann Strauss

Wines to Try Next Time

Wines to Try Next Time

Wines to Try Next Time

Wines to Try Next Time

> *... wine is life,*
> *and my life and*
> *wine are*
> *inextricable.*
>
> M. F. K. Fisher

Wines to Try Next Time

Addresses & Contact Numbers

Name	Name
Address	Address
Phone	Phone
Fax	Fax
E-mail	E-mail
Name	Name
Address	Address
Phone	Phone
Fax	Fax
E-mail	E-mail
Name	Name
Address	Address
Phone	Phone
Fax	Fax
E-mail	E-mail

Addresses & Contact Numbers

Name	Name
Address	Address
Phone	Phone
Fax	Fax
E-mail	E-mail
Name	Name
Address	Address
Phone	Phone
Fax	Fax
E-mail	E-mail
Name	Name
Address	Address
Phone	Phone
Fax	Fax
E-mail	E-mail

Addresses & Contact Numbers

Name	Name
Address	Address
Phone	Phone
Fax	Fax
E-mail	E-mail
Name	Name
Address	Address
Phone	Phone
Fax	Fax
E-mail	E-mail
Name	Name
Address	Address
Phone	Phone
Fax	Fax
E-mail	E-mail

Addresses & Contact Numbers

Name	Name
Address	Address
Phone	Phone
Fax	Fax
E-mail	E-mail
Name	Name
Address	Address
Phone	Phone
Fax	Fax
E-mail	E-mail
Name	Name
Address	Address
Phone	Phone
Fax	Fax
E-mail	E-mail

Addresses & Contact Numbers

Name	Name
Address	Address
Phone	Phone
Fax	Fax
E-mail	E-mail
Name	Name
Address	Address
Phone	Phone
Fax	Fax
E-mail	E-mail
Name	Name
Address	Address
Phone	Phone
Fax	Fax
E-mail	E-mail

Addresses & Contact Numbers

Name	Name
Address	Address
Phone	Phone
Fax	Fax
E-mail	E-mail
Name	Name
Address	Address
Phone	Phone
Fax	Fax
E-mail	E-mail
Name	Name
Address	Address
Phone	Phone
Fax	Fax
E-mail	E-mail

Wine Labels & Miscellanea

Wine Labels & Miscellanea

Wine Labels & Miscellanea

Wine Labels & Miscellanea

Wine Labels & Miscellanea

Wine Labels & Miscellanea

Wine Labels & Miscellanea

Wine-Tasting Terms

Wine-Tasting Terms

There is no shortage of terms used to describe wines. To get you started, here is a short list of some of the more conventional descriptors.

Acidity

The right amount of natural acidity is an essential component of fine wine, giving it a fresh, zingy flavour. Lack of acidity can be detected by a general flabbiness (the taste of butter comes to mind), a lack of vitality and, sometimes, by a watery finish. Too much acidity leaves a sharp, tart, sour flavour in the mouth.

Aroma

The scent that derives specifically from the grape of a wine. A wine's aroma can be distinctly varietal – such as the grassy, grapefruit aromas of a Sauvignon Blanc – or just plain grapey as opposed to the bouquet, which stems from the wine's development in the bottle.

Astringent

A dry, mouth-puckering effect caused by high tannins extracted from the skin of the grape or from the wood.

Balance

The best possible relationship between a wine's key components: fruit, acidity, tannin and alcohol.

Big

A wine that is full of flavour and high in alcohol, tannin, acidity and extract.

Wine-Tasting Terms

Body

The weight of a wine on the palate. A wine's body is normally related to its alcohol content and extract. The higher the alcohol content and extract the greater the body.

Bouquet

The pleasant odours of a wine that has developed well in the bottle over time.

Clean

An absence of any foreign or off odours in a wine.

Corked

An off, oxidized, objectionable smell in a wine. Not to be confused with the smell of cork.

Crisp

A white wine that is firm and refreshing.

Dry

An absence of residual sugar. A wine in which all grape sugars have been fully fermented.

Fat

A full-bodied wine that is rich in extract and alcohol and normally of a lower acidity. Big and round on the palate but without much nerve or vitality.

Finish

The aftertaste. In a well-balanced wine, the finish is normally long and distinctive as opposed to short and poor.

Wine-Tasting Terms

Fruity

An attractive, fleshy flavour in a wine that derives from perfectly ripe grapes.

Green

A wine with unripe, raw fruit flavours is often described as having a green flavour.

Hard

A wine with too much tannin and acidity and not enough charm.

Heavy

A robust wine with high amounts of alcohol and extract. More than just full-bodied.

Light

A wine with less body and low alcohol. A desirable feature in wines such as a German Riesling from the Moselle or a Beaujolais.

Long

A reference to the length of time during which a wine's aftertaste lingers in the mouth.

Oaky

Wines fermented or aged in oak with a distinctive toasted, vanilla, buttery flavour are often referred to as oaky.

Plonk

An inexpensive, simple, everyday wine. Can be a derogatory term for wine that is of undistinguished quality.

Wine-Tasting Terms

Soft
An overused term that denotes a mellow wine with no rough (acidic or tannic) edges.

Spicy
A term used to describe a wine's rich, herblike aroma and flavour. Sometimes described as peppery.

Sweetness
The sugar content of a wine, which can range from zero in a dry table wine all the way up to 10 for late-harvest dessert wines, such as an icewine or Sauternes.

Tannin
A natural preservative that is extracted from the grape skins during a wine's fermentation process. Over time, as a wine matures and mellows, the tannin will precipitate out of the wine. The presence of tannin dries the roof of the mouth.

Woody
An undesirable taste imparted by wine that has been kept in the cask too long.

Notes

Notes

Notes